Designing

HOLLYWOOD
HOMES

Exterior terrace of Aniston home in Beverly Hills (see chapter "The Tonight Show")

Designing
HOLLYWOOD
HOMES

MOVIE HOUSES

STEPHEN SHADLEY

with PATRICK PACHECO

foreword by DIANE KEATON

RIZZOLI
NEW YORK

New York · Paris · London · Milan

For Dorothy Shadley,

WHO TAUGHT ME TO BELIEVE IN AIR CASTLES

Contents

Movie Houses

A hat rack in the townhouse of Soon-Yi Previn and Woody Allen (see "Interiors and Nostalgia")

Courtyard at home of Ryan Murphy and David Miller (see "Path of Desire")

Foreword

BY DIANE KEATON

Steve and I met long before we worked together on my many homes. I think our first encounter in the 1970s in New York City was through a mutual friend, an artist named Mike Balog. My first impression of Steve was that of an eclectic artist. Not only was he a successful off-Broadway set designer, but also a runway photographer for the *Los Angeles Times* and a painter. For me, it was a meeting of the minds.

Once, I got up the nerve to ask Steve's opinion on an eight-hundred-square-foot New York apartment I was thinking of buying. He rejected it, telling me he wasn't ready. Persistent, I never gave up on my dream of collaborating with him. Years later, I asked again. This time it was a sprawling yet neglected house on the Hudson River. Thankfully, he agreed. Together we had lots of ideas; I, of course, had my own. Steve listened and more importantly, he understood and then implemented them. This marked our first of many projects together and more importantly was the birth of our "forever friendship."

Our bond continued. Next, an old ranch in Southern Arizona. There, under the desert sky, we watched Howard Hawk's western movies at night and during the day hit desolate antique stores as inspiration for my newly acquired home. From the 1980s to today, we have renovated and reimagined forgotten Spanish Colonial homes throughout Los Angeles. Through it all, Steve's contributions have been remarkable and invaluable.

Recently we were driving together on the old Pasadena Freeway and realized that, as kids, we had lived just minutes from one another; me in Highland Park and Steve in Eagle Rock. It made me think about those two kids with dreams, in such close proximity to one another, and an unexpected friendship that has endured forty-plus years. Although he's lived much of his life in New York, he spent many years growing up in Southern California appreciating the history and lore of the West.

The movies and Steve's early experience as a scenic artist in the Hollywood studios helped shape his approach to design. I think he sees things cinematically, which brings a sense of narrative and drama to his work. Whether it is an architectural project or an interior design creation, the common thread is his ability to listen, to absorb and to create.

As an admirer of Steve, I share his vision and deep love of the American Southwest, Los Angeles and Hollywood. Now it's your turn to enjoy the collected stories presented in these pages.

I think of his journey as a nod to the past and a promise for the future.

Detail from Diane Keaton's home in Bel Air (see "On a Mission")

My career as an interior designer has been both accidental and inevitable.

Accidental because while I had plenty of ambition I had little confidence. That is, until I met a well-known designer, Bob Bray, who provided key encouragement in the early days. As well—and fortuitously—by that time I knew an extraordinarily gifted woman, Diane Keaton, who would generously share her talents in collaborations that continue to this day.

Inevitable because I had a mother, Dorothy Shadley, who convinced me I could do anything I set my mind to. And also that, from an early age, I had a passion for movies which opened within me a world of wonder and imagination.

Looking back, I can trace the beginning of my love affair with Hollywood and homes to the Sunday afternoon when, at my insistence, my family piled into our 1953 matte blue Pontiac Chieftain to search for Walt Disney's house in Holmby Hills. We had recently moved to Los Angeles from St. Louis, Missouri, and it was only the year before that Dorothy had taken my brother John and me to see Walt Disney's *Sleeping Beauty*. To describe it as a profoundly seismic event in my life would be an understatement. I begged my mother to endure the long bus ride downtown to see it six more times, and, even now, many decades later, I look with happiness at a newspaper ad for the film that I carefully cut out and preserved for posterity.

As we drove along Wilshire Boulevard from our modest home in Inglewood toward Holmby Hills, I'm not sure what I expected to find. Perhaps a glimpse of the Great Man himself watering his lawn? But, like millions of others who buy those maps of stars' homes hawked on corners, movies represented a romance in life that we just weren't living at the time and they sparked a desire to go to a place where it was real and attainable. Just to breathe the air and to be in the proximity of it was enough.

Those same fantasies were nurtured as well by my high school art teacher, Clay Beale, who was a first cousin to Montgomery Clift and who regaled us with tales of his visits to Pickfair, the legendary home of Douglas Fairbanks and Mary Pickford, designed by Wallace Neff. Years later, my fascination would continue when my friend Tim Hawkins and I sought out the homes of Greta Garbo and Katharine Hepburn in New York. I suppose, even on a subconscious level, I must have believed that men and women who lived their lives in front of the camera had to bring that glamor into their homes as well.

I got my foot in the door, so to speak, into the glorious world of film when I landed a job as a scenic artist at 20th Century Fox. As I helped paint the New York cityscape for *On A Clear Day You Can See Forever*, I became fascinated with film production design—the painterly approach to color, texture and composition. I realized then how cinema affects the way we see the world around us and, sometimes, how we actually want to live in it. Films come and go each year and yet the stories they tell and the places they portray continue to live in our minds and spark our imaginations. They are the popular reflection of our common experience and visual lexicon.

I came face to face with someone who could touch the public in just that way when—following 20th Century Fox and a stint with *Disney on Parade*—I moved to New York to pursue a career as an artist. One summer day, I opened the door of my Chinatown loft to greet Mike Balog, a friend and fellow artist, who'd brought along a guest: a young woman with the charm, humor, curiosity and total self-effacement which would make America fall in love with her a year later.

Diane Keaton had yet to become Annie Hall but, as we got to know each other, I admired in her what I would later discover about the many film artists—Jennifer Aniston, Ryan Murphy, Matthew Modine, Woody Allen, and Robert Altman—with all of whom I'd later collaborate on homes. Like many of her peers, she was a huge romantic and fearless when it came to putting herself "out there." Diane met life on her own terms. She would take on enormous projects and bring everything she had to the table, pushing the limits with tremendous passion. I could match her on passion. I couldn't—and still can't—match her energy.

After we met, our friendship grew. We took in the occasional movie or art show. I watched as she became more and more famous through her remarkable achievements and she saw me through an evolution from aspiring artist to designer. That began when a friend, the actor Michael Murphy, asked me to design sets for an Off-Broadway show, *Rats Nest*, which he was directing. I accepted. Shortly after, the same people involved in the play decided to renovate a restaurant from a casual Eastside neighborhood hangout, Dr. Generosity, to a more elegant establishment to be dubbed Camelback and Central.

I was not the first choice to design the restaurant. Bob Bray, then a celebrated designer, was. But he generously passed the baton to me. Whatever insecurity I had about my first major design job was erased with his confident assertion: "You can do this. Besides, I'll have your back every step of the way." How Bob had more confidence in me than I had in myself is just one of those little miracles in life to which the only response is gratitude.

The restaurant was a big success and drew a glittering clientele, Diane Keaton among them. So I was more confident when some years later Diane asked me and my design partner at the time, Richard Gillette, to take a ride up the Hudson River from Manhattan to Snedens Landing to renovate a house. A year later, it would be featured in *House & Garden* and formally launch a career that had been steeping for years through a mania for all things Disney, to the workshops of 20th Century Fox, to a colorful stint with *Disney on Parade*, and, along the way, lucky and

What holds true for all of these chapters is how each of these homes reflect their owner's love of story. They breathe it. They live it.

Our collaborations in sketching those narratives are drawn from the sum total of our respective experiences. So what follows is my story, their story and the story of our partnerships, informed by the history of film and architecture and animated by passion, wit, joy, maverick taste, and theatricality. Collaborations as accidental and inevitable as my career has had the good fortune to be.

Bob Bray Fire Island, NY, 1980s

STEVE

(Clockwise, from top) Dorothy Shadley, wardrobe, *No, No, Nanette*, Los Angeles, 1972; Stephen Shadley, high school; Stephen, at ten, with brother (at right), John, Eagle Rock, California; A name tag from Disneyland; Stephen at his animation board.

THIS IS THE **ONLY** THEATRE

IN THIS AREA, where you can see all wonders of this magnif NEW motion picture in TECHNIRAMA 70— and **ONLY HERE**, can experience the sensation its glorious music in full **STEREOPHONIC SOUN** as Walt Disney visualized its perfect presentation

WALT DISNEY'S

Sleeping Beauty

TECHNIRAMA 70.
process lens by Panavision
TECHNICOLOR.
and
FULL
STEREOPHONIC
SOUND

APR 62

ADDED ENCHANTM

EMY AWA
WINNER!
live Acti
rt Subje
DISNE
D CANY
echnicolor
inemaScope
Stereophon
Sound
0 A.M.
ic Momen
P.M.

Newspaper clipping, 1959, St. Louis; Stephen and
friends at 20th Century Fox studios, 1969; Richard
Gillette and Stephen, 1990; polaroid of painted

Rats Nest, Camelback & Central, Barragán Pink

In early 1979, my friend the actor Michael Murphy asked me to design the set for an Off-Broadway play he was directing. Even though I had never done such a thing, I didn't hesitate to sign on. By then, it had been over two years since I'd arrived in New York and I was not exactly setting the world on fire as a visual artist. *Rats Nest*, a five-character play about the denizens of a neighborhood bar, provided a diversion, especially because the cast featured my old high school pal, Tom Nardini, and introduced me to an actress, Susan Lange, who would become a lifelong friend and colleague.

I created a sleazy hangout of peanut shells and sawdust for the play which was based on the experiences of its authors, Neil and Joel Cohen, who worked at Dr. Generosity, an Upper Eastside bar. After the surprising success of *Rats Nest*, they decided along with Barry, the owner, and Murphy, to renovate the bar into a trendy Upper East Side restaurant. To design the place they smartly went after a good friend of mine who'd come downtown to see *Rats Nest* and hang out with us: Bob Bray, who was among the established stars of the emerging industrial high-tech style.

Bob—Oklahoma-born, tall, enthusiastic, and wickedly funny—suggested to the Cohens that they instead think outside the box for their designer. And outside the box was...me.

"What do you mean, me?" I told Bob. "I'm not a designer."

"You can do better than a lot of stuff out there," Bob replied. "And I'll be looking over your shoulder."

With more than a little trepidation, I took up the challenge, enticed to some extent with the prospect of a $4,000 fee and a $4,000 restaurant tab. Needless to say, I relied at almost every moment on Bob, who was in every sense of the word Dr. Generosity him-self. With one stroke, he could show me what was possible, lending an air of monumentality to modest spaces, tearing down walls and discovering vistas that no one else could imagine. Bob's point of view was clear and concise, often a distillation of what I wanted but which hadn't occurred to me as yet. By the same token, he knew I was a good student. I listened intently and took his suggestions to heart.

Located on the corner of 73rd Street and Second Avenue and still graced with a long, vintage chestnut bar, the stripped-down room seemed to demand an atmosphere of high-tech serenity fused with old-fashioned warmth. Keeping everything rather spare, I created a partition covered in industrial carpet to separate the bar from the softly lit dining area. I painted the entire place in a glossy and matte shade of mauve and indirectly lighted the walls with simple quarter spheres. A massive plate glass window fronting the street featured a snazzy sandblasted logo by Neil's girlfriend, April Silver, announcing the name of the newly re-christened restaurant: Camelback and Central, so called after an intersection in Phoenix, Arizona. The restaurant was an immediate success, quickly gaining a starry clientele. It didn't take me long to chew through my tab.

Coinciding with the development of the restaurant was an unexpected foray into the pages of *Gentleman's Quarterly*, again thanks to Bob. He was visiting me in the Chelsea loft to which I'd moved from Chinatown when he suddenly piped up, " "I can get your loft into *GQ* if you paint that wall pink."

"Pink? PINK? What are you talking about?" I replied, looking at the large white curved wall that separated the office from the rest of the apartment.

"And we're going to call it Barragán Pink," he added, after the legendary Mexican architect Luis Barragán, famous for indulging in vivid colors.

That was certainly something I'd never considered. But my trust in Bob, not to mention the giddy prospect of actually being published, soon had us painting the wall in "Barragán Pink." The magazine, as Bob well knew, was doing a story on color in the environment and, sure enough, my newly painted wall was to be featured. Not yet satisfied and with the *GQ* shoot looming, Bob paid for industrial carpet to be installed in my bedroom and went on the search for fine art with which to decorate the loft. So there we were, carrying a five-foot bronze Bruno Almeida sculpture down 6th Avenue from his studio. In short order, the piece was joined by a Giacometti sculpture as well as a conceptual artwork created by my friend Mike Balog. The text accompanying the *GQ* article described me as "...a jack of all trades, designer, painter and photographer."

"Designer"? Seeing that in print came as something of a revelation. As unschooled and inexperienced as I was, it had never been part of my personal lexicon.

But after *Rat's Nest*, Camelback and Central, and a Barragán Pink wall, I supposed I'd arrived at the designation, thanks to people as giving and supportive as Bob Bray.

"Stephen Shadley, designer."

I had to admit there was a nice ring to it.

"What are you getting involved with this lunatic for? She's the biggest degenerate in the world. She'll steal your cigarettes. She'll put her hands in your pants and steal your tips. I'm telling you . . ., she's an out-patient."

Shelter West presents
A new play by Neil and Joel Cohen

RATS NEST

Directed by Michael Murphy

CAMELBACK & CENTRAL

AT 73RD & 2ND ▶ 212/249-8380

CAMELBACK & CENTRAL

Dinner

APPETIZERS

CHICKEN LIVERS sauteed in sherry with grapes and almonds 2.95

SKEWERED PORK TENDERLOIN with peanut sauce 2.95

ASSORTED COLD SAUSAGES with potato salad vinaigrette 3.25

COLD SEAFOOD ANTIPASTO squid, shrimp, scallops, scungilli 3.50

SOUP OF THE DAY 1.95

HOUSE GARDEN SALAD vinaigrette or danish bleu cheese dressing 2.50

FRESH TOMATO, MOZZARELLA, and BASIL 2.75

COLD SEASONAL VEGETABLES with puree of eggplant and garlic 2.75

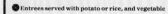

ENTREES

CAPELLETTI 6.25
Veal and chicken filled pasta with light tomato sauce and romano

ROASTED HERBED CHICKEN 6.95

BREAST OF CHICKEN 7.25
Lightly sauteed with tomato, basil, and walnuts

COLD POACHED SALMON 8.50
Cucumber and mint

GRILLED SWORDFISH 8.75
With herb or anchovy butter

STUFFED VEAL CHOP 11.50
Stuffed with spinach, gruyere and prosciutto

ROAST DUCK 9.95
With port wine and currant sauce; apple and prune stuffing

PAILLARD 8.95
Sirloin of beef grilled with shallot butter

SHELL STEAK 12.50
Broiled, or pan fried with green peppers, onions and pimento

VEGETABLE OF THE DAY .... 2.25   BAKED POTATO SKINS AU GRATIN 2.25

● Entrees served with potato or rice, and vegetable

DESSERT

CHOCOLATE SILK PIE 2.50		AUSTRIAN PLUM CAKE 2.50
FRESH FRUIT TART 2.50		KEY LIME PIE 2.50
ICE CREAM 1.50		SHERBET 1.50
CAPUCCINO 1.50		COFFEE .... .75
ESPRESSO 1.25		TEA .... .75

MOVIE

HOUSES

A SENSE OF DRAMA

DIANE KEATON / SNEDENS LANDING, NEW YORK

*I*n the late 1980s, Diane Keaton, Carol Kane and I were driving up the West Side Highway of Manhattan to look at a house in Snedens Landing, a Hudson River enclave about an hour from the city. Since I'd met Diane ten years prior, the times I had spent with her—at movies, museums, flea markets and the like— were always instilled with a sense of adventure. This was no exception.

The difference, though I didn't know it at the time, is that this foray into the unknown would mark the beginning of a lifelong collaboration with her on the whole nature of what is *home*. Early on, we'd explored a couple of her previous residences together, but I never felt I was good enough to collaborate. Since then, however, I had designed a set for an Off-Broadway play, *Rats Nest*, and renovated a hangout into a chic, Upper Eastside restaurant named Camelback and Central. I'd also joined forces with the talented Richard Gillette, a fellow designer. So when Diane's invitation came to do "a couple of things" with Snedens Landing, we were more than ready to work with her. I thought it would be fun. That turned out to be quite the understatement.

That afternoon, Diane, Carol and I peered into a white clapboard, split-level, ranch-style house dating back to the '40s with dark woods setting off wall-to-wall carpeting and old sofas covered in Mexican blankets. It was not unlike a Ramada Inn room.

"I haven't got much to spend," said Diane.

Carol was doubtful. "Diane, a sofa could be thousands."

Diane replied, "Really?"

Money was not the object. It never was with Diane. Being a creature fascinated with design, she was all about Iconoclasm. Innovation. Reinterpretation. Once she was engaged on a project, she was totally committed and that extended to spending whatever she thought was needed. The transformation she had in mind was light, clean, bold, and elegant. The house lent itself to a Mid-Century Modern look. But she also set out to break the norms.

"I don't like any style that is too rigid so that you can't do whatever you want," she said.

We both loved that period because it was one of the great moments of experimental design, a radical change to how people experienced their domiciles. There was a roster of great talents reinventing what furniture could look like, including Charles and Ray Eames, Marco Zanuso, Alvar Aalto, and Paul Frankl. Their work was comfortable but held daring shapes and forms that nobody had ever seen before.

To create a strong graphic environment, Diane suggested that we paint the entire place white, a stark envelope to contain the furniture. As a photographer, she knew that the place would photograph well and that the whiteness would tie all the disparate rooms together. When it came to the columns and beams that delineated the dining room from the living room, Richard's painterly approach was key. We painted an exaggerated white faux wood grain over the actual wood, which, coupled with the step between the rooms, created a "proscenium" look that gave the place a strong theatrical flair. An anticipatory sense of drama began at an entry with black and white squares and a rare plywood chair designed by Frank Lloyd Wright.

To these choices, Diane brought her own fearless aesthetic. She had been born in California and would return to her home state. But it was in New York where her career came alive and gave her a certain confidence, especially when it came to design. As a movie star, Diane was very visual and embraced the graphic severity of mid-century modernism with an enthusiasm that I admired. She absolutely loved the process and the thrill of discovery and the learning that went with it. Curious doesn't begin to describe her. *Focused* does.

As we embarked on a scavenger hunt for pieces that would fill the house, Diane was on the look out for furnishings that could be adapted to her particular vision. If something had never been done before, she was all the more for it. Take the vintage linoleums we used on the bathroom vanity and on the kitchen cabinets and doors. I'd always liked the user-friendly material. It's waterproof, durable and there is a tactile softness that has a give to it. But it can also make for arresting visuals—which was the case of the optical patterns that we chose.

Diane was equally enthusiastic when we came across a couple of amoeba-shaped natural cork tables, which we stained white and placed together in the living room, a configuration that gave them a fresh and unexpected resonance. At the counterintuitively named Skank World in Los Angeles, I found a Henry Moore–like floor lamp that resembled a sinuous woman. In a variation on a party drunk playing with the proverbial lampshade, I suggested to Diane that the piece seemed to demand a hat. I designed the shade upside down on the lady in question. The whimsy tickled us. This breakthrough became one of the first signatures of our collaboration.

The Lady of the Hat ruled a retinue in the living room that included Paul Frankl sofa and chairs, deep and low, with strong, square lines. *Clunky* might be a good word to describe them; to Diane, they were simply wonderful. We paired them with an Alvar Aalto cowhide chair from the early '30s. She had little patience for anything that was too precious or fussy. Unsurprisingly, Diane was thrilled with anything quirky. Richard and I spent all afternoon walking along the Hudson River, recovering driftwood which we then modified into handles for the bedroom dresser.

When Richard and I came across a couple of lamps inspired by the sputnik satellite at Second Hand Rose in Manhattan, we knew that they would immediately appeal to Diane. After all, we'd both come of age in the era of *The Jetsons, Forbidden Planet,* and *Star Trek*. But I wasn't sure she'd want to live with them. The lamps were massive— over five feet in diameter with 140 spokes each—and most probably had once graced a hotel lobby or airline terminal. They'd go with the anthropomorphic Charles Eames chairs in the dining room, not to mention the space age-y Marco Zanuso chairs in the bedroom. But would they be too dominant? When we returned with Diane to the store, she loved them on sight.

We sent them out to be refurbished and the electricians hung them. One evening, I then screwed in hundreds of white Christmas tree bulbs at the ends of the spokes. Afterwards, I manned the dimmer switch, turning the lights up and down, which made the sputniks appear to expand and contract with each adjustment. The cosmic sensations put me in a frame of mind that was pure 1960s.

I was struck by a thought: "Oh, man, am I high?"

No doubt about it. My first collaboration with Diane had broadened my imagination in a way that was truly *galactic*.

A MAVERICK'S MOVEABLE FEAST

KATHRYN AND ROBERT ALTMAN / UPPER WEST SIDE, NEW YORK

*I*n 1989, when Richard Gillette and I were brought in to collaborate with Bob and Kathryn Altman on their duplex apartment on New York's Upper West Side, we were given a couple of mandates. Bob's was akin to why he loved jazz: "It doesn't have a beginning or an end. It's a moment." Improvisation is what he, as a director, always brought to his films. That is also how Bob liked to live. Kathryn wanted the spaces to be "warm and seductive." Which was an apt description of her. A former showgirl, Kathryn was a tall, charismatic and fiery redhead with a personality to match. How else could she keep up with a husband whose mischievous nonconformity had rocked Hollywood with such films as *M*A*S*H**, *Nashville*, The Long Goodbye, and *McCabe & Mrs. Miller*?

Coming to the East Coast, the Altman's love of theatricality drew them to the Pythian, a building, flamboyantly designed by Thomas Lamb, whose movie-set exterior exulted in Art Deco Egyptian Revival, complete with pharaoh-like figures, polychrome columns, gargoyles, and griffins. Created in 1927 as a temple for the Knights of Pythias and converted by architect David Gura into condominiums, the ten-story edifice had been described in the AIA guide to New York City as "an opium smoker's

Stephen with Bob Altman, 1980

dream." Given Bob's affection for cannabis, the place was more than appropriate as the Altmans' urban foothold on the East Coast.

What greeted us when we entered the apartment was, if not trippy, at the least disorienting and somewhat confusing. The perimeters of the rooms disappeared as we were immersed into a world created by hanging glass panels, 18-feet high and silk-screened with an eclectic array of images, including a smiling Nubian woman, a Biafran child, an American farm worker, and J. Robert Oppenheimer, the physicist who helped develop the atom bomb.

Bob had discovered a trove of the panels in Montreal while shooting his 1979 film, *Quintet*, a post-Apocalyptic nuclear thriller, starring Paul Newman. They had been among the remnants of Expo '67 in the Canadian pavilion, which was themed "Man and His World." Bob loved them and, after wrapping up the film, chose twelve of the forty-four panels to take with him. Once the Altmans were ensconced

at the Pythian, the glass panels were airlifted through the windows of the apartment and installed amid an austere environment of steel, neon and glass.

They had a mesmerizing, Altmanesque effect. As often with his movies, the glass panels gave you a disorienting sense of overlapping dialogue. You could look at them but also see through them to other glass panels so there was a constant visual and experiential exchange going on. It was an illusory and moveable feast. As sunlight filtered through the apartment, elements from the panels, a disembodied eye here, a hand or hat there, were projected onto the walls or ceiling. Even the expressions on the faces seemed to change.

"It's a little spooky," said Kathryn with a laugh.

Our first order of business was to bring continuity to the 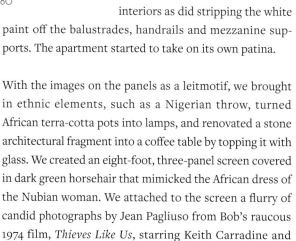 sensory jumble, a painterly approach which would make the place homier, and the addition of textiles and furnishings that would make it more comfortable. Richard placed sheets of German silver leaf on the ceilings of the living room and the dining room, which reflected the light but which also picked up the grainy patterns on the silk-screened panels. It helped to soften and warm the interiors as did stripping the white paint off the balustrades, handrails and mezzanine supports. The apartment started to take on its own patina.

With the images on the panels as a leitmotif, we brought in ethnic elements, such as a Nigerian throw, turned African terra-cotta pots into lamps, and renovated a stone architectural fragment into a coffee table by topping it with glass. We created an eight-foot, three-panel screen covered in dark green horsehair that mimicked the African dress of the Nubian woman. We attached to the screen a flurry of candid photographs by Jean Pagliuso from Bob's raucous 1974 film, *Thieves Like Us*, starring Keith Carradine and Shelley Duvall. Adding a piquant touch was a sweet shot of Kathryn as a young girl, affectionately pinned by Bob to the screen.

Bob and Kathryn were well matched. They'd met in 1959 when she was recruited to be an extra in *Whirlybirds*, a television show he was directing and which, as a boy, I'd watched faithfully at the time. Bob took one look at the

long-legged Kathryn Audrey Reed, who'd been featured on Broadway in *Earl Carroll's Vanities*, and was smitten. She liked to tell the story that he approached her on the set with the worst—or best—pick up line.

"How are your morals?" he asked.

"Not so good," she replied. "How about yours?"

They married later that year.

Ever the auteur, Bob could direct the proceedings in the apartment with taste and discernment but Kathryn would make it happen. They were both open to our suggestions and, just as Diane Keaton had been about her place at Snedens, were especially delighted when it was something they'd never seen before. They loved to entertain, and their duplex was often filled with their motley and glamorous crew of friends. They immediately cottoned to our idea of a large built-in banquette upholstered in an emerald green mohair fabric originally designed for the La Scala opera house. Kathryn loved the color, which was a match for her green eyes. They sparkled when accompanied by her easy, throaty laugh.

But the appeal that the fabric held for her was also due to its theatrical origins. So in addition to the Mario Bellini black leather club chairs into which Bob could fold his lanky frame, she loved the two enormous turn-of-the-century Portuguese banquet tables, which had come from a theatrical prop warehouse. With griffins adorning each leg of the tables, they were in sync with the ornate exterior of the Pythian.

Bob's affection for props lay more in the Eskimo sculptures and Southwestern masks, mementoes from his far-flung travels. Also in his collection were small metal airplanes bought from a 21-year-old kid in San Francisco and whom he also commissioned to create the model helicopter he'd used in *M*A*S*H*. Bob, who had been a pilot during World War II, was infamous for his combative and maverick attitude toward the film studios. While he could be gruff, he was never less than fun and agreeable with Richard and me. He did, however, have a puckish sense of humor. He loved to watch something go wrong.

We got a huge dose of this subversive trait as we were putting the finishing touches on the apartment. Bob and Kathryn were away on a film set and due to come back on the following day. Earlier in the process, Bob had asked us to create a large saltwater aquarium. We had contracted a New Jersey firm to create it and, much to Bob's horror, they had filled it with traditional coral. At Bob's direction, we retrofitted the entire tank with crystal towers and clear

cubist architecture so that the colorful, Day-Glo yellow Tangs would stand out in all their phosphorescent glory. We had worked tirelessly to put everything together in time for Bob and Kathryn's return, when I got a call from Marie, the housekeeper. The aquarium had burst and salt-water was leaking into the apartment below. We ran over but there was little to be done except to mop up and contain the damage. It fell to me to make the call to the Altmans. I was beside myself. "This is the worst thing that could have happened!" I wailed into the phone. Bob listened patiently and finally said, "How are the fish?"

I replied, "The fish, Bob, unfortunately didn't make it." There was a pause on the other end.

Finally, he said, "That's sad."

Neither Bob nor Kathryn ever held it against us and we actually had a good laugh about it. After Bob died, Kathryn re-stocked the aquarium with fish she named after the Dionne quintuplets. One afternoon, she told me, "I can make the fish kiss one another."

"What do you mean?" I asked.

Kathryn tapped the glass three times. Sure enough, the fish swam through their Cubist world toward the glass and kissed each other. Again and again. Kathryn got her warm and seductive world, after all.

ADOBE DREAM

DIANE KEATON / AN HOUR FROM TUCSON, ARIZONA

*D*iane Keaton has never been in a Western, yet she loves them. It was fun watching several with her in the late '90s, including John Ford's *The Searchers* and Howard Hawks's *Red River*. And just outside the window was the mesquite-and-cactus landscape that the films were celebrating. We were in southern Arizona, where Diane had found a modest and charming 1930s ranch house about an hour from Tucson and I was helping to add some simple touches she had in mind.

We hung out there for a week or so at a time, traveling to Arizona's hot Sonoran Plateau from Los Angeles in her vintage Defender Land Rover whose air conditioning only sometimes worked. Packed into the car with us were her dogs, Josie and Brownie. Diane rescues dogs the way she rescues houses. Looking back on that adventure now seems like a dream, partly because this was my first introduction to the flat and dry landscape of the Southwest. The house itself was remote with a long dirt road. You even had to drive across a riverbed to get to it.

More than any of the other houses we worked on together, this simple adobe structure was a family affair. Jack and Dorothy Keaton, Diane's parents, had a vacation home in the area and after her father died, she had continued to visit her mother and her sister, Dorrie, there. Diane's love of the Southwest had come from her father who was passionate about its geography, flora and lore. On their outings, the family would often camp out or stay in an adobe hacienda.

When Diane saw this sweet little house on one of her frequent visits, she was hooked. And, once she told me about it, so was I. Her enthusiasm was always infectious. Even though by this time I had begun my own business, there was nothing formal about our arrangement. We were like two grownup kids just having fun.

Diane didn't have any grand illusions about the house. It had once been part of a larger cattle ranch and Diane, respectful of its origins, had hired a local carpenter to do the renovations. The elderly sisters, who'd owned the place prior, had added a 1950s extension, which needed to be better reconciled to the original structure. Reflecting her love of light and shadow, Diane came up with the smart idea to open up the rustic, dark rooms to more light by inserting glass into the panels of all exterior doors. It was a modernist touch but retained the original character of the place with its contrasting white walls, dark ceilings and wood trim.

The area had been settled by a resilient people, building their homes from whatever materials nature had provided. One of these was adobe from which the uneven walls of the house had been made. They gave the house a pure and understated feeling. Another was the color of the red concrete floors. It came from the local tradition of mixing animal blood into the concrete to strengthen it, though over time it became pocked with air bubbles. "It's fun to see the age on things," said Diane.

Out back, there was a low brick wall, which defined a charming garden enclosure. Nearby were two enormous mesquite trees, which stood like sentries to the property. With those as my markers, I designed a pool and then extended the brick wall to surround it, the trees, and the entire backyard. We created a hardscape of concrete for the courtyard and tinted it red to match the floors of the house.

Taking her cue from the trees, Diane found a massive old mesquite table for the enclosure, representative of the expansive and clean lines with which we styled the house. Fusing the local architecture with the spare geometry of twentieth-century design—Arts and Crafts pieces filled the dining room and a screened-in porch—the Arizona house was the beginning of Diane's fascination with a Western aesthetic, which would lead to a passion for Monterey furniture.

On this project, I learned firsthand just what an indefatigable shopper she could be. Since we were in the middle of nowhere, we'd clamber into the Defender in temps hovering around a hundred and haunt the antique stores and flea markets of Tucson, Bisbee, and Phoenix. Whenever I was prepared to pack it in, Diane was always ready to go to "just one more." On one of these trips, I found a floor-stand ashtray in the form of a saguaro cactus, native to the area. She at first resisted—she didn't think she needed it—but the shape was just too endearing. I wouldn't let her leave the store until she bought it.

When Diane found something she loved, she'd collect it in multiples. By this time, she'd become a fixture at the Rose

Bowl Flea Market, spending hours mulling over vendors' tables with her foldaway cart in tow. It was there that she started collecting such items as clown paintings (which she'd one day arrange into a book), concrete bears, and old photo albums with wood covers, which we arranged on the shelves of the ranch house.

She had dozens and dozens of these memento books, each individually made, as though they'd come out of somebody's wood shop. Some of the covers had small cutouts in which had been placed snapshots or decorative ephemera like drawings or pictures of cacti. She was especially drawn to those with Southwestern or California motifs. I could understand Diane's fascination with them. For one thing, collecting in multiples allows you to have a broader understanding of an art form and what it is trying to express. For another, although each was unique, there was a stylistic unity to them. More importantly, each told a human narrative, the cherished memories of the people they'd once belonged to, and Diane was, of all things, a lover of humanity first and foremost. This was as true in her personal life as in her role as a designer.

Our habit at the end of every evening—after I'd made a simple dinner of pasta and salad—was to take Brownie and Josie for a walk down the long dirt road. I remember one night was so dark you could barely see your hand in front of your face. We carried a flashlight, just in case, but almost never turned it on. In the ineffable quiet of the night, broken only by the occasional howl of a coyote or grunt of a wild Javelina pig, the sky was so ablaze with stars that it seemed as though we were walking in a dream. Which is how I remember those early times and that simple, lovely and isolated house.

COPPER FEVER

CARI AND MATTHEW MODINE / GREENWICH VILLAGE, NEW YORK

As the son of an itinerant drive-in movie manager, Matthew Modine was looking for what he called "permanence" when Richard Gillette and I met the actor and his wife, Cari, in 1989. Matthew was thirty and in the full flush of stardom, having by then received raves for *Birdy, Full Metal Jacket, and Married to the Mob*. That meant lots of time on film locations. So when he finally alighted, he wanted a perch that would be a calm and steadying oasis. Since, as a child, I had lived in over a dozen places before I bought my first house, we had that in common as well as a love of Arts and Crafts design and the purity and sense of order that came with it. We brought all of that to bear in the re-design of the Modines' nineteenth-century carriage house in a Greenwich Village mews.

Unlike Diane Keaton's home in Snedens Landing or Robert Altman's Upper West Side duplex, we were confronted for the first time with having to transform the spaces, which due to a 1970 renovation had been left as a labyrinth of unrelated rooms with a newly-dug basement and a bedroom addition at the rear of the house. That lack of cohesion presented a challenge but a welcome one. Five years into my partnership with Richard, we may have evaded the straitjacket of a particular signature but we loved fixing problems.

Among the first things we did was to add staircases, a more formal one descending into the basement and, later in the renovation, another leading up to a light and airy garret, which we added at Matthew's suggestion. The house was expanding, as was their family. Boman, their son, was three and Cari was pregnant with Ruby, so, in addition to their master bedroom, the kids' rooms would be on the first floor and the garret. Matthew told us that he wanted his children to live in a house that was simple and uncluttered. "That way," he added, "the emphasis is on the inhabitants and not on the house or furniture."

Given the Modine family's star quality, it wasn't likely that they would be upstaged by our designs, which were open, light and as airy as possible. To that end, we removed a wall to put in a delicate network of gridded screens that could act as handrails to the freestanding staircases. The rectangular shapes established a Mondrian-like leitmotif we carried throughout the house, constructing a layered series of grids with wood frames and glass block to define the rooms. Slowly and organi-

cally, the house began to take on a flow and a unity of interconnected rectangles throughout.

Matthew, who is a gifted painter, was an enthusiastic and energetic collaborator. He had dug the basement to the house, which should tell you something about his ambition, since Manhattan lies on a bed of nearly impenetrable mica schist. On top of that, he'd sneak into Washington Square Park in the dead of night and plant trees. Very Johnny Appleseed.

Matthew was away filming *Memphis Blues* for a good part of the time, but we spent hours on the phone with him and the fax machine would be humming at all hours of the night with his sketches and ideas for the renovation. He loved the process and his contributions were smart, well-articulated, and always came back to a spiritual reverence for home.

Matthew Modine with Bob Altman on the set of *Streamers*, 1984

That extended to the Arts and Crafts style that we were both so enamored with. Unlike most people of his age, Matthew was not afraid of wanting everything to be pretty. William Morris, the prime purveyor of the Arts and Crafts philosophy, would have approved. "Have nothing in your houses that you do not know to be useful, or believe to be beautiful," he noted. There was no greater follower of that motto at the time than the New York craftsman, Gustav Stickley, who named one of his chairs after Morris and whose humanistic aesthetic was totally in sync with the simple lifestyle Matthew craved. He believed, as Morris did, that the house you live in can change the way you are.

The clean, sharp lines of the furniture also reflected our Mondrian theme. Arts and Crafts, which was a strong reaction against the machine age and was an endorsement of the nobility of craft, gave us the first modern

furniture. But what we attempted to do was a "jazz riff" on what was then a very popular genre, incorporating those elements in a way that people hadn't seen before. So the furnishings were often Stickley-style with our own unexpected and disparate elements. With their soft-colored slag glass, the light fixtures looked like Stickley but were more of an impression of the style than a copy. In this way, our modernist approach was in sync with the individuality that was key to Arts and Crafts, a movement in which highly personal touches were exalted.

Matthew and I also bonded over our affection for copper with its malleability and warmth. Mine stemmed from a childhood where in grammar school I hammered a copper image of a horse's head; his from the summer he spent retrieving the copper gauge wire from speakers at shuttered drive-ins. "I've had copper fever ever since," he told us. To assuage that, there was copper throughout the house, from assorted fixtures to the copper leaf on a wall, to the plates, which disguised the Scandinavian radiators.

What was important in designing this "urban tree house" was to bring the outside in as much as possible. What fulfilled that mandate beautifully was a wall opposite a view of wisteria winding its way around an iron balustrade. We commissioned Carlo Mori, a young Florentine craftsman, to execute a design of an impressionistic landscape in Venetian plaster stucco. We carried the leaf motif, omnipresent in the house, in gold, ochre, and brown, above which Carlo created bas-relief leaves, which would create shadows as sunlight moved through the windows. He had done a magnificent job.

When Matthew saw the wall, he said, "It's beautiful! Stephen, it makes me think of that moment in the movie when Bambi's mother says, 'Bambi, wait! You must never rush out in the meadow.'"

To this Disney-mad aficionado, it was music to my ears.

ROMANTIC OBSESSION

DIANE KEATON/BEVERLY HILS, CALIFORNIA

A fragment of a tile can tell a lot about Diane and her priorities. This particular turquoise-colored piece was not even from one of her homes. She'd snuck in and grabbed it from the demolished remains of a Beverly Hills house that had once belonged to Jimmy Stewart.

"They just can't be tearing that down," she told me, regretting each and every other architectural gem that had met the wrecking ball in Southern California. Such sacrileges had led Diane to be a major force in the Los Angeles Conservancy, fighting the losing battle to save the Ambassador Hotel but engaging in others that were more successful. Where a realtor saw a "tear down," Diane saw faded beauty.

Both of us having grown up in Los Angeles, one of our mutual pleasures was to ride around the city, admiring the houses of such renown architects as Rudolf Schindler, Cliff May, and Irving Gill. As we passed the fortress-like water and power municipal buildings, Diane would muse over what it might be like to live in one of them.

Her romance with the storied past of her native city blossomed when Diane spied a house a few blocks from the Jimmy Stewart site: a 1926 beautiful Spanish Colonial Revival designed by Wallace Neff. The emotional power of its provenance was compounded by the fact that we got to know its owners, Ambrose and Aurelia. Then in their nineties, this lovely couple had been only the second owners of the house and their affection for it was palpable.

This was the first time that I was dealing with a house created by a notable architect and, along with Diane, I was careful to respect and honor that legacy. From the beginning, our mission was clear. Everything got reduced to its essence. "I want to be pure about this," Diane said. "The simpler the better."

Neff's forte was to adapt the elements of Spanish Colonial with a 1920s modernist touch. The house, with its layered influences, reminded me of the gorgeous biennial issues of *Architectural Digest* that re-published the magazine's original stories of the homes of Hollywood stars. These included Mae West's Art Deco building on Ravenswood, the Santa Monica beach cottage shared by Cary Grant and Randolph Scott, and the Beverly Hills home of Charlie Chaplin and his then-wife Paulette Godard, who, by the way, was rumored to have had an affair with Neff. The pages, invariably in black and white, conjured a fantasy of film gods and goddesses bringing onscreen glamor into their homes.

While maintaining the original form of the house and the integrity of the rooms, we brought more light into it, inserting a glass panel into the heavy wood front door and adding windows in the living room.

While retaining the original tile floors in the entry and living room, we introduced bleached white cement floors in the kitchen and family room. I enlarged the kitchen by combining three small rooms, and exposed a tiny window to the street that had been hidden under an outside stair. By making these spatial changes, I gave Diane an envelope into which she poured her brilliant and varied ideas. Given her wide-ranging visual lexicon, she was always fearless and confident in her choices. As she was an inveterate researcher, I would often find Diane in her office poring over dozens of three-ring binders into which she'd catalogued images that had captured her imagination.

In bringing the house back to its original style, Diane was creating a loving and romantic narrative of her California heritage, expressing more fully two recent obsessions: Monterey furniture and Western art of the early twentieth century. The furniture, with its clean, graphic lines, strength and warmth, fit perfectly into the rooms. Each vintage piece was set sparingly so a tableau of just a chair and a lamp became a modern way of evoking the past. To Diane, an object's shape was just as important as its context, and Monterey furniture hadn't been used in quite this manner before. In fact, the style was not widely popular when Diane began collecting it; her passion for it moved the market. The price of the furniture skyrocketed.

Diane's interest in all things Western led her to an appreciation of the work of Maynard Dixon, a sexy, renegade artist whose 1923 painting, *The Grim Wall*, took a place of prominence over the fireplace. With its grayed-out tonalities and large swaths of simple colors, the nocturnal work was more graphic than textural and echoed the silhouettes of the Monterey furniture. Not surprisingly, Diane was taken, as was I, with his biography. Born in Fresno to aristocratic Virginia confederates, he was a San Francisco illustrator until his life changed when he

took a horseback ride through Arizona and Mexico. From these travels would spring a bold and mysterious style that would distill the West to its essence, placing humans in his paintings, if at all, as subservient to nature.

That motif was dramatically carried on in the master bedroom in one of the most provocative photographs in Diane's impressive collection: David Wojnarowicz's image of buffaloes going over a cliff to certain death. Depicting a Native American hunting custom called a "buffalo jump," Wojnarowicz had pointed his camera at a portion of a large diorama at the National Museum of American History. Paired with a Monterey buckaroo chair, the intriguing work resonated not only with the Western themes of the house but also with the personality of its owner—beautiful, romantic and tough, all at the same time. Dorrie Hall, Diane's youngest sister, once said to me, "Diane is the most unsentimental sentimental person I know." Sentimental in the passion, energy and fervor she pours

into her houses and their contents; unsentimental in that she can let them go without a backward glance. It is a testament, however, to her extraordinary taste and unerring instincts that when she does sell them, the subsequent owners rarely change anything about them. That was also true of the Neff house.

Someone who paid tribute to Diane's design savvy was none other than Wallace Neff Jr., the architect's son. A chronicler of his father's work, he contacted us about paying a visit and, though Diane was going to be out of town, she asked me to show him around. He marveled at what we'd done. Afterwards he took me to lunch at the Bel Air Hotel and I had the great pleasure of talking to him about the man who'd occupied and stimulated our imaginations for months and months. He expressed his admiration in a grateful letter to Diane, which she shared with me. The letter served as a fitting capstone to the entire project.

OSCARS GREENROOM, 2009

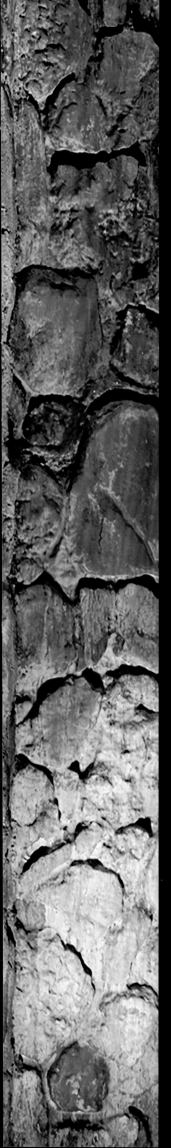

STARRY, STARRY NIGHT

DESIGNING GREEN ROOMS FOR THE OSCARS AND EMMYS

EMMY GREENROOM, 2004

"Hello, everybody. This is Mrs. Norman Maine!"

In 2004, I was standing on the stage of the Shrine Auditorium in Los Angeles, recalling the final scene in the 1954 classic, *A Star Is Born*. It was on that very stage that Judy Garland, as Vicki Lester, reminded the glittering audience that she was still the proud wife and widow of her washed-up movie star husband, played by James Mason. It was for me, a lover of vintage movies, a pinch-me moment.

The venue had been chosen as the site of the 56th Emmy® Awards and I had been invited to design the *Architectural Digest* green room, where the stars and presenters would hang out until they were called to the stage. It was an honor I was to repeat the following year as well. I was then in the midst of collaborating with Diane Keaton on her homes and I took my inspiration for both green rooms from the work we had been doing: a variation on Spanish Colonial for the 2004 Emmys and a California Mid-Century Modern look for the following year.

I was mindful that my job was to create an environment that would soothe jangled nerves, since award shows are most often a jumble of high anxiety, competition, and tedium. I hoped that the Mission style of the '20s and '30s—with Navajo rugs, hardwood floors, Monterey furniture, and plein-air paintings—would invite people to kick back and relax in an atmosphere of Old California glamor.

The next year, I took my cue from the Case Study houses of California—that experimental period from 1946–1966 during which such architects and designers as Richard Neutra, Charles and Ray Eames, A. Quincy Jones, and Eero Saarinen built homes to express the Mid-Century Modern ethos of post-war America. Echoing that aesthetic, I filled this green room with glass tables, Eames chairs, and sculptural lamps that looked like musical clefs. These were set against an illuminated photographic backdrop of nighttime Los Angeles that I borrowed from J. C. Backings, where I once worked as a scenic artist. It gave the space an illusion of "altitude," so to speak, letting the stars imagine they were looking out over a city most of them had set out to conquer.

In 2009, the altitude got even thinner when I was asked to design the Architectural Digest Greenroom for the 81st Annual Oscars. That year Jennifer Aniston was a presenter and she might have felt at home in the green room. After all, it had been inspired by the house on Hillcrest that I had just finished for her, with its clean and simple lines, massive walls of stone and expanses of glass. I designed a dropped ceiling and had a scenic shop simulate stone walls, adding garden seats, lounge chairs, an eleven-foot sofa, and a shag rug to cover the wood floors. I stuck to neutral shades, knowing that color would be added by the evening gowns of the women. A sleek stone bar was on hand for those who might need a little Dutch courage before fanfare summoned them to the podium.

The 2009 ceremony was, as usual, a dazzling pageant— *Slum Dog Millionaire* won Best Picture. But there was a somber moment when a posthumous Oscar was presented to the family of the recently deceased Heath Ledger for his performance as the Joker in *The Dark Knight*. Sometimes life lived at that altitude takes a tragic toll.

OSCARS, 2009

ARCHITECTURAL DIGEST
GREENROOM
AT THE
81ST ANNUAL ACADEMY AWARDS®
DESIGNED BY STEPHEN SHADLEY

ARCHITECTURAL DIGEST
Hollywood at Home

ON A MISSION

DIANE KEATON/BEL AIR, CALIFORNIA

When Diane Keaton was young, she took trips with her family to visit the missions dotting the California coast, spiritual symbols of the early history of the state, which had been settled by Spanish explorers and their band of Franciscan friars. I never knew her to be traditionally religious, but she loved the rituals and iconography of Christianity. If we passed some poor animal killed on the road, she'd make the sign of the cross out of respect. There are crosses on the graves of her dogs, the many strays and rescues, and is a recurring motif in much of her jewelry.

The romance that missions exemplified attracted her to a 1920s Spanish Colonial Revival house that sat on an acre of land in Bel Air, California. I loved that it had once belonged to the film director Peter Bogdanovich, who'd extended hospitality there to a down-on-his-luck Orson Welles. Diane loved its shape and the feeling of safety and calm that the interior courtyard gave it. She even loved just how much work the renovation was going to take since the house had been remodeled so much that there was little left of its original charm.

So out came Diane's three-ringed binders filled with visual references and ideas jotted down in her angular handwriting. Looking through them, we searched for inspiration on how best to re-structure the kitchen and dining areas, the cavernous living room, and the three cramped rooms on the upper floor. The family room, swimming pool and cabana took on added importance, since by that time her family included eight-year-old daughter Dexter and four-year-old son Duke.

Some of our ideas also came from our frequent road trips, jaunts to the Santa Barbara Courthouse, a marvel of Spanish Colonial Revival, and the any-Spanish-style home we could get into. Diane arranged a trip to San Diego to visit with architect, Wallace Cunningham, a disciple of Irving Gill, who in turn had apprenticed with Frank Lloyd Wright. In his company, we toured several of Gill's historic structures, which helped form our plans for repurposing the vintage Bel Air house with modernity and a graphic sense of space. Gill was a master at paring design down to the minimal basics, such as simple fireplace mantles, stucco walls, concrete floors, a unity of materials, and lots of arches.

Even before our tour of Gill's homes, Diane had been fixated on arches, having seen them as a common element in the Catholic missions. Given their structural beauty, arches were the perfect complement to provide passageways from the kitchen and breakfast area to the dining room and also to demarcate the kitchen and its tiled bar. In the kitchen, we installed a massive 1950s chrome O'Keefe and Merritt range, which Diane and I had found in typical fashion. One day, we were driving around Culver City in Los Angeles, when suddenly she piped up, "Omigod! Omigod! Steve, stop! There's this stove in the window. We have to go back!" I knew enough by that time that nothing, but nothing, escaped her eagle eye.

Previously, Diane had steered away from vibrant colors, relying instead on bold blacks, whites, and browns to emphasize the strong graphic elements of furnishings and architecture. After installing a custom brown tile in the kitchen and family room, she decided it needed more color and doggedly set about collecting hundreds and hundreds of vintage California tiles from swap meets, stores, vendors, and eBay. Finally there were enough for us to rip out and replace the brown tiles in the kitchen and the family room as well as to add them to the cabana fireplace and the trim of the pool. Paired with equally colorful pieces of pottery, plates and vintage dishtowels, the spaces joyfully evoked the enduring Mexican influence on California's heritage and history.

The arch also played a major role in the master bedroom. At first, Diane was more concerned about her children's bedrooms, being happy to take a small and unimposing room near them. But I came up with the idea to create a master suite by extending the second floor above the garage. It gave me the opportunity to design a massive arched niche framing the large Monterey-style bed, which I had designed for the earlier Wallace Neff house. I added a long balcony that ran along the interior courtyard, providing another connection from her bedroom to the master bath. I've always loved creating multiple ways of entering and leaving rooms.

Below the master suite, we had carved out an office from what had been Bogdanovich's screening room. As a nod to its previous use, Diane had placed a large vintage sign spelling, "FILM," atop the desk that had been refashioned from an old factory table. Its broad surface suited her need for spreading out from end to end her changing collections of visual references. Behind the table was a bulletin board that was just as large, every inch covered with her ever-mutable narratives and collages. In fact, she had approached this project as though she were directing a film. No detail was too small to escape her attention.

The living room, with its Monterey furniture and Western paintings by the likes of Maynard Dixon, Frank Tenney Johnson, Edgar Payne, and Carl Oscar Borg, was meant to evoke a waiting room in a train station. It was a bow, of sorts, to the transience of so many elements in Diane's life: the nomadic life of an actor, the culture of missions as a way station for pilgrims, the inevitable fact that as much as she loved this house, she would move on from it at some point.

But while Diane was there, she celebrated its interiors with warmth and light—literally. On one occasion, for a party, she took it upon herself to outline the roof of the house and its walls with hundreds and hundreds of "luminarias." These candles, set inside sand in a paper bag, are a Southwest custom meant to light the way of the Christ Child to one's home. Whatever the religious significance, the dazzling luminosity was in sync with a motto that Diane had painted on the massive arch above the kitchen, a paraphrase of a Robert Frost quote: "Home is a place where when you knock on the door they have to let you in."

OR THEY HAVE TO LET YOU IN

INTERIORS & NOSTALGIA

SOON-YI PREVIN AND WOODY ALLEN / UPPER EAST SIDE, NEW YORK

*T*he phone rang. It was Diane.

"Steve, Woody is looking for somebody to help with a new place in New York and I told him about you. You may get a call."

I was thrilled at the prospect of working with Woody Allen, though a little nervous. I had bumped into him at a couple of parties with Diane, but had never really gotten to know him. I was so intimidated in his presence that I rarely got out more than a few sentences. And Woody's not exactly what you'd call outgoing.

Diane continued. "Now, Steve, if you get this, he's the easiest person in the world. He's good that way."

Easy? Really? Like everybody else, I knew Woody as a genius filmmaker who'd parlayed agitated neuroses into an art form through the characters he played. I suppose I expected Alvy Singer of *Annie Hall* to show up at our first meetings—cynical, unsure, questioning and skeptical. Instead, I found a consummate gentleman who had clear ideas, a strong sense of narrative, and a keen grasp of visual composition. At the same time, he was always open to suggestion and dialogue. From the beginning, he was direct. Explaining to him how I worked, I added, "If you decide that you want to go ahead with me—." He interrupted. "I do want to work with you. Diane recommended you and that's enough for me."

Woody, his wife, Soon-Yi Previn, and their two daughters were then in the middle of moving from their massive townhouse in the East 80s of Manhattan and searching for suitable digs in the neighborhood. He asked me to tag along whenever a realtor gave him a tip and we eventually found a well-proportioned gem on a leafy street with a beautiful staircase, a proper vestibule, and a tranquil garden. It had good bones. Soon-Yi gave her approval as well. Occasionally the taskmaster, she looked out for Woody and his preferences.

Given that the new home was smaller than their former one, a good deal of their possessions went into storage. I spent a lot of time in the "editing room" with Woody, reviewing the inventory—furniture, lamps, paintings, collectibles, samplers—most of which was tethered to a romantic past. How Woody chose to live was reflective of the movie worlds he created, at least the early ones set in an idealized New York. His taste placed a sophisticated gloss on a folksy Americana far from the frenetic Brooklyn of his youth. Despite his love for the Scandinavian director Ingmar Bergman, the style was more Norman Rockwell than Edvard Munch.

As I pushed around furniture, Woody stood at the entrance to each room, looking to "frame the shot." The story he was telling was one of nostalgia, bathed in warm reds and yellows. An old spa chair in cracked leather here, a hooked rug there, a collection of nineteenth-century samplers above the bed, needlepoint pillows in the library. The Neo-Jacobean blue dining room was a cool departure. I was accustomed to looking at a room with my clients from many different angles, experimenting with the different perspectives. Woody, however, immediately knew the viewpoint that was right for him. I would mention if I thought that a Ruscha or Rauschenberg would give a lift to the traditional approach. But Woody's instincts were excellent.

A product of his generation, Woody's lifelines were his jazz albums, the typewriter he'd used since high school, and the simple desk on which he spun comic gold. For someone who'd gained legendary status as a writer, Woody's choice to forego a third-floor study and instead park his desk in a corner of the bedroom could only be chalked up to humility. He gave the study instead to Soon-Yi. "I like working in the bedroom," he told me, adding that he practiced his clarinet there. "For Soon-Yi, my playing is torture."

I converted a sturdy Napoleon III architect's drawing cabinet to house his turntable and well-worn albums. They played while Woody wrote on legal pads, often on his bed, before he pecked out his scripts on the 1951 Olympia. When I asked him where he got the ribbons, he said, "I gotta guy." Above the desk, I placed a charming needlepoint of a busy beehive. "It's a metaphor for his mind," I thought to myself.

Less expected were a couple of primitive treasures that I immediately loved: two large naïve paintings of Mickey Mouse and Minnie Mouse. Woody had never let on that he was particularly interested, as I was, in All Things Disney, despite the brief, animated scene in Annie Hall, in which Alvy reimagines Annie as the Evil Queen in Snow White. Woody told me that he had bought the nostalgic paintings on wood from Greenwich Village dealers who sold antiques out of their home. He couldn't explain exactly why he liked them—intuition guided Woody more than most of my clients—but he had no intention of letting them go, even after Robert Iger, the head of Disney, called my office looking to procure them.

The notion that floor coverings could solve the unusual layout of the entry hall prompted an afternoon visit to Stark Carpets in the D&D building. Woody was familiar with the showroom, having shot a pivotal scene there for his 1978 film, *Interiors*. Geraldine Page was brilliant as Eve, a troubled decorator in the Bergman-like drama set in rooms of austere and chilly beauty—so very unlike the all-enveloping warmth we were then in the process of creating. We came away with a number of rugs which we had fun arranging and re-arranging, overlapping them across the entrance. Soon-Yi watched us. "This looks like a mish-mash," she said. "I knew I shouldn't have left you two alone." She wasn't far wrong—though I wouldn't have called it a mish-mash. After all, in the movie, *Interiors*, Eve observed about decorating, "It's not an exact science. Sometimes you just have to see it and get a feel for it."

As the project was winding down, Woody called me over to the library window and pointed across and down the street to a brownstone that had served as Alvy Singer's apartment in *Annie Hall*. He had shot both interiors and exteriors there almost thirty years before. Woody always advised the art directors for his films to give the homes of the characters he played the same lived-in comfort which surrounded us. "This has always been my favorite block in New York City," he said. As a setting sun bathed the brownstones in soft light, it was hard to argue with that.

OHANA

*J*en named the Beverly Hills house on which we first collaborated "Ohana," a Hawaiian term which means "extended family." That should tell everything you need to know about her. Those personally close to Jen take precedence over virtually everything, including her career and its astonishing, attendant fame.

The demands on her time are legion, so when she didn't show up for our first meeting I was resigned but disappointed. I thought it was my one chance at the project. By the time I got back to where I was staying in Pacific Palisades, there was a follow-up call from her estate manager, Phill. "Stephen, how fast you get back to the house?" he said. "Jen can meet you there after all." Despite the fact that it was rush hour in Los Angeles, I think I must've catapulted over the 405 Freeway and up to the house, which Hal Levitt designed in 1970. The view overlooking Los Angeles was breathtaking. On a clear day, you could see Catalina Island in the distance.

As I spoke with Phill inside the house, the door suddenly opened and Jen came running down the hallway and threw her arms around me. "I'm so sorry!" she exclaimed. "I'm just glad that we could meet today." Drawing back, she looked at me. "So, tell me, what do you think about the house?"

Stephen's drawing of a proposed, but never built, house for Jennifer Aniston, 2012

That warm embrace was a prelude to what would become one of the most entrancing and pleasurable experiences of my career. Having just ended her first marriage, Jen was eager to turn the page and it was clear that a new chapter of independence was being written, in part, through a house she clearly loved. "When I first walked through those doors, I knew I was home," she said. I was taken by her enthusiasm and, as a designer, excited by the

opportunity: the architectural gem, the abundant resources, a committed collaborator. I felt like a director about to embark on an epic production. What was Ohana to Jen was nirvana to me.

She once described show business as "nutty, brilliant, wonderful and hard," so I wasn't surprised that the first word she used to define her goal for the house was "zen," a sea of tranquility amidst the bustle of her life. The notion of home as sanctuary is endemic among stars, who must constantly contend with their lives under scrutiny. Understandably, among her favorite features of the house were the fourteen-foot, impenetrable bronze doors.

The place was in a state of disrepair and among the first structural changes we made was to extend the roof line by six feet, not only for protection from the elements but for a shaded and sensuous Balinese feeling. We carried through that island allure with an open-air anteroom to the entrance hall: a koi pond over which we created a travertine bridge. While the wood-and-bronze walls and gates encircling the house created a fortress-like exterior, Jen wanted the interior to convey warmth and comfort to her extended family.

Like Mary Pickford, a previous "America's sweetheart" with a legendary domain, Jen was intent on making her home a social hub where she could host parties from four to four dozen and more. We worked hand-in-glove burnishing the house's old-fashioned Hollywood glamour with an overlay of contemporary and casual elegance. "I can just imagine the Rat Pack stopping by," she said. "Someone playing the piano, and people are laughing in the next room."

I could imagine that, too. The period of the house suggested referencing classic Hollywood tropes of open spaces, trellised room dividers, shag carpeting, expansive drapery, and sliding glass doors, all emblems of a seductive lifestyle. I didn't care if they were fashionable or not. Like everything else, popular ideas are re-cycled and re-invented from strength to strength, decade to decade. What mattered was how they complemented the modern elements I had in mind.

As an architect, Levitt was drawn to textures and Jen responded enthusiastically to my modifications of those elements. That started with the original, knotted,

wrought-iron screens, which I re-fashioned to frame the travertine bridge in the outdoor vestibule. For the interior envelope, I used various but consistent materials that conveyed a sense of theatrical drama worthy of its owner. Smooth plaster walls contrasted with others of Bel-Air stone further set off by floors of Brazilian cumaru wood, the same as the extended eaves. A wall of massive bronze panels, echoing the entrance doors, stood guard at one end of the dining room. The ubiquitous travertine stone was varied by color and cut; for example, red for a table, pale, soft and cloud-like for the entire master bath.

But the "yellow brick road" into this Oz was the travertine passageway that ran from the entrance, continued unbroken to the expansive lanai, and then out to the terrace and pool. The lanai was not only the key transitional room, protected from the weather and connected to the house on three walls, but it was also the space that best reflected Jen's spirited and earthy personality. Though she grew up in New York, the daughter of actors John Aniston and Nancy Dow, Jen exuded the "fine, fresh, fierce" energy that Katy Perry sings about in *California Girls*. The lanai epitomized the playful indoor-outdoor essence of the house and yet at the same time a thirty-foot metal mesh curtain could be drawn across to temper the mid-day sun and give a sense of calm enclosure.

Next to the lanai, the focus of the home naturally bent towards the kitchen and dining room, where Jen could entertain up to twenty-four guests on a table hewn from a single slab of Claro walnut. (In the spirit of conservation, the wood used in the house had been cut from fallen trees and solar panels had been installed on the roof.) When it came to entertaining, Jen's generous spontaneity demanded a certain flexibility. At one point, I suggested that perhaps an extra one or two of the dining room chairs should be ordered. Without missing a beat, Phill said, "Let's make that six." Parties for two dozen could suddenly double or triple in number.

To handle the social demands, we created a kitchen-within-a-kitchen. The main one featured a wood-fired pizza oven and wine room. It was there that Jen eventually found herself spending time visiting and laughing with a handful of friends over snacks and drinks. But right next door was another full-on, stainless steel chef's kitchen which was, for good measure, sound-proofed. At times, the level of detail lavished on the project—from the

wrought-iron cabinet pulls to Robert Motherwell's 1963 *Throw of Dice, No. 17*—brought to my mind the oft-quoted observation about Hollywood homes: "What God could do if he only had the money."

Although we spent wisely, I didn't feel designing that home was driven by budget. It was an attempt to get it right and to pay homage to a beautiful structure on a spectacular site. Setting the tone was my first outing with Jen to a modernism show in Santa Monica where we both fell in love with a unique 1960s German fruitwood piano. (It would feature prominently in an article on the house in *Architectural Digest*.) We later took in the annual New York Armory show together. To say that she was the most popular attendee there would be an understatement. Yet, Jen never seemed to be affected by her staggering level of fame.

One of my fondest early memories was when, on a trip to New York, she invited me to dinner at Nobu in Tribeca. In the course of the meal, we talked about all our plans and ideas for the house. Afterwards, we came out of the restaurant to the bodyguards and paparazzi, which are so much a constant in her life. It was a beautiful summer night so she took my arm and said, "Let's walk a little."

As we made our way north, the photographers waned and security stayed well behind. For almost three miles, there was just the two of us, as she walked me back to my loft in Chelsea.

THE SECOND TIME AROUND

DIANE KEATON/BEVERLY HILLS, CALIFORNIA

THE·EYE·SEES·WHAT

3

The public knows Diane Keaton for her movies as well as for her unique personal style, which, immortalized in *Annie Hall*, started a fashion trend. At home, she is no less stylish but usually barefoot, even when that home is a construction site and the result has been many broken toes. That free-spirited approach was the key for our renovation of a simple house on North Roxbury Drive in Beverly Hills, the fifth in our series of collaborations.

The Spanish Colonial style house had been designed by Ralph Flewelling in the 1920s and Diane's purchase of it in 2006 was the second time around. We'd seen it years before and she'd even made an offer. But another house caught her attention and she backed out of the deal. When it came back on the market three years later, she had no second thoughts. She was especially taken with the enclosed and nicely proportioned courtyard. It gave the feeling of being in the contemplative quiet of an early California mission—even though the house was just one block from Sunset Boulevard.

A speculator had bought the house and done extensive renovations. Some good: an enlarged kitchen out of which a family room could be carved so that her two kids, Duke and Dexter, could romp. Some bad: several disparately designed fireplaces (one with a faux coat-of-arms insignia) and an entrance that had been bumped up from one story to two, a boxy room as ungainly as it was unwelcoming.

Diane loves big spaces. No ceiling can be too high and no space too large. After all, she fantasized about what it would be like to live in a Los Angeles water and power building. But it didn't take her long to size up the cavernous entrance and suggest a clever remedy. "Steve, why don't we make this into a library?" I loved the idea. For one, it was unorthodox. What house has a library for an entrance? For another, she had a vast amount of books, many over-sized volumes devoted to architecture, art and photography, her big passions—though, surprisingly, not as many about the movies.

To make the entrance warmer and more engaging, we vaulted the high flat ceiling, put a clerestory window above the front door for added light, and lined the walls with deep bookshelves that made the room feel cozier. We installed a rolling stepladder and, as the house neared completion, I would often find her on top of it, arranging and re-arranging the books, alphabetically and by topic. She ringed the walls around the bookshelves with the maxim, "THE EYE SEES WHAT THE MIND KNOWS," painted in capital letters.

What Diane knew about the house was that all five of the fireplaces had to be remade to suit the house's Spanish heritage. What eventually worked was a sketch I made of an arched brick opening surrounded by white stucco plaster and topped by a graphic squared-off mantle. But then the search was on, along with Diane's quest to find just the right brick. Weeks later, a brown oversized one ended the hunt and we modified the same design on all the fireplaces throughout the house, including the bedroom and kitchen. The same brick served as the building block for a big apron off the front door and planters around the house. When Diane finds something she loves, she likes to use it over and over again. The vocabulary may be limited but the choices are not.

The reassurance that comes from repeated elements came into play in the loggias surrounding the courtyard, a symphony of dark beams, white stucco walls, arched doorways, brick floors and black iron grilles framing the windows. Simply furnished with Monterey benches and chairs, the spaces recalled for Diane "the ache of romance" of the missions and historic California hotels she visited with her family when she was a child. The courtyard itself, with its gurgling fountain and entrances and exits to the rooms, gave the house a theatrical flair. It also made its owner feel safe and protected. "You're walled in by the shape of the house," she told a writer. "Everything looks inward which is actually very soothing. It's like you're creating your own home. Your own world."

In all of our collaborations, Diane was intent on creating her own worlds; some might even call them sets. A lifetime of mapping out her longings on bulletin boards pinned with images torn from shelter magazines, architectural blogs and websites was always geared toward creating what she called "the perfect California home." One that was never far away from the collective impulses and dreams of the artists who originally built the houses she bought and resold. Diane could perfectly articulate to me the ideas that she had in her head. Translating them into concrete, wood, and glass was another matter. Perfection can never be reached. But she came as close

to it as humanly possible. In an introduction to her book *California Romantica* she expressed her manifesto: "The secret wish for the ambiguity of drama, the dark side of romance, the bittersweet lie of perfection."

What stands as a testament to her relentless drive is the fact that the people who later purchased the houses we worked on changed very little about them, if anything. They might have been created, to a certain extent, as showcases of ideas. But they were always functional and organic. In other words, livable. Like the Old Masters who sketched the skeletons of their subjects before draping them in brightly colored robes, Diane was as meticulous about the less visited areas of the house as those on display. In the recesses of her bedroom closet at the Roxbury house was a museum-worthy installation of her hats, dozens upon dozens of brimmed hats, top hats, caps and berets.

We finished off the renovations by covering the driveway and courtyard in DG—decomposed granite, a favorite material of hers because it was often used at the California missions. The rough golden beauty comes with a disadvantage. Everyone was telling us, "Don't use it. It's dusty and dirty. It can make a mess, especially if women are wearing high heels."

Diane wasn't concerned. "Don't worry, that's so not me," she replied.

THE TONIGHT SHOW

JENNIFER ANISTON/BEL AIR, CALIFORNIA

The first time I saw the massive 14-foot red lacquered doors that were the entrance to Jen's house in Bel Air, I immediately knew that their days were numbered. But what to do? Inspiration can come from many quarters and, in this case, it came from a most unlikely source: *The Tonight Show Starring Johnny Carson.*

One night at my loft in Manhattan, I was watching an homage to the legendary entertainer and among the featured clips was footage of the show's premiere. There, in black and white, was a screen behind Carson's desk and the nearby sofa perforated in a beautiful motif. Recalling the set from nights spent watching the show in my youth, I grabbed the TV remote and rewound the footage back and forth, letting a solution to Jen's front door seep in. "What a perfect pattern to sandblast in bronze," I thought. I grabbed my phone and took screen shots. I sent them to Jen whose enthusiastic reaction matched mine. With her own history of talk show appearances, she loved the provenance as well as the design itself.

On this second collaboration with Jen after the process of designing her previous home in Beverly Hills, I found someone now more confident in her choices and sense of style. She knew how she wanted to live: casually elegant with a muted color palette, straightforward and simple textiles and fabrics, classic furnishings in graphic shapes, and rooms with a connection to the open air of Southern California.

Johnny Carson, 1962, *The Tonight Show* premiere

"I'm all about cozy and comfort, " Jen said. Sexy and fun were also part of her design lexicon.

This structured informality was to be layered on a mid-century house designed by A. Quincy Jones and which had been modified later by the architect Frederick Fisher. The stark modernist ambiance was a little too cool and minimal for Jen's taste. So the first order of business was to introduce organic materials of texture, substance and depth—wood, stone, bronze—which would add a tactile,

welcoming warmth to the place. As Jen put it, she wanted her home to reflect "old world meeting new world."

Getting the flow right started with the living room, which was a large and unstructured space. Knowing Jen's penchant for entertaining, I came up with the idea of an imposing bar as the theatrical anchor of the room. My design featured large walnut panels set apart in a spacious alcove carved from what had been an adjacent storage space. I loved the idea that you could walk into and around this intimate space and fix yourself a drink (an informal touch which was always a hit with guests). The off-white suede and bronze bar stools provided a perch on which to hang out. At the other end of the room, I created a symmetrical surround of blackened bronze for the wood-burning fireplace. You could slip into both the bar and fireplace areas but you could still feel a part of the social activity at large.

Jen embraced sensual décor throughout the house—shag rugs, silk carpets, suede headboards, leather chairs. But a sexy ambience is mostly determined by the people who inhabit a room and her guest list more than filled that bill. The trick was to create contexts that were conducive to intimate conversation. I did this in the living room through the placement of three sofas, creating a number of corners to which guests could retreat for a chat. For the kitchen, which featured one of Jen's favorite elements, the pizza oven, I designed an island counter, always a popular place to congregate and where Jen, no stranger to multi-tasking, could toggle between visiting with friends and working at a nearby desk.

The Asian calm, which was so much a part of our first collaboration, suffused the new house as well, but with more eclectic flourishes that demanded a harmonious layering. Jen's office was a case in point with its modernist Don S. Shoemaker "power" desk, 1930s French leather lounge chairs, Tiffany lamp, and a large tapestry evoking the classical Far East. I took care in selecting fabrics to show Jen because she had a keen, almost mystical connection to them, whether vintage Indonesian textiles or plain Belgian linens. "They feed my soul," she said.

Also providing a quiet refuge was the master bath with its deep stone tub and a floor-to-ceiling, wall-to-wall window. It looked out on a walled-in Zen garden, which I replicated on the opposite side of the house off the dining room. A press of a button retracted the glass panel to add the sybaritic pleasure of bathing amid soft breezes or a cooling rain from the outside. Lest things get too relaxed, however, I created just off the bath a capacious closet, lounge, salon, and dressing room for fashion fittings, a constant in the life of one of America's busiest stars.

Unimpressed with her celebrity was a trio whose comfort was paramount: Dolly, Sadie, and Clyde, her dogs. For them, I'd dug into my past and recalled the beanbags I'd made for the first house I'd ever owned in Laurel Canyon. I deviated from the usual teardrop design of these 1960s' icons and made them in a tall drum shape. Once filled with Styrofoam beads, I could flip them on their sides and they formed a comfortable seat. Covered in fake fur, they were the cat's pajamas in canine spoiling—or even a spare seat for a human.

When Jen sold the Beverly Hills house, the new owners had asked to buy the entire contents. So she took with her only those possessions to which she had become most attached. That included the dog beds as well as her bedside lamps by Philip and Kelvin LaVerne, Robert Motherwell's *A Throw of the Dice, #17*, a sculpture of a sixteenth-century Chinese deity, and a striking bronze figure of a crane, lit from within.

Jen was quite fond of the crane, giving it a place of prominence in both homes. I later found out that, in Asia, the crane is considered a mystical and holy creature, representative of justice, good fortune, happiness and eternal youth. It sounds to me like a good symbol to keep around wherever you find yourself in life. But especially if you find yourself in the insistent glare of Hollywood stardom.

PATH OF DESIRE

RYAN MURPHY AND DAVID MILLER / PACIFIC PALISADES, CALIFORNIA

I n the fall of 2013, I got a call from a close friend. "My God, Stephen," he said, "the set for *The New Normal* looks like a house you designed."

I tuned into the sitcom about a gay couple raising a family and, sure enough, I recognized it as the Bel Air house I had renovated for Diane Keaton five years earlier. There were the same vintage tiles in the kitchen, the courtyard in front of the house, and a living room that nostalgically evoked a train station waiting room. The producer-director Ryan Murphy had chosen to film his new series in the house that had remained just as Diane left it. I decided to write Murphy a note expressing my delight and also to register my admiration for his other groundbreaking work, which by then included *Nip/Tuck, Glee,* and *American Horror Story*. I received no response.

However, three years later, Ryan and I stood in the kitchen of his Beverly Hills home on Roxbury Drive—another house on which Diane and I had collaborated and which he'd purchased from her. He'd called to gauge my interest in working with him on a new house he'd just purchased. After visiting the site, he'd invited me to join him at the home he shared with his husband, David Miller, and their two kids. I hadn't been there since Diane had left and everything was much the same. I reminded him of the note I'd written after seeing *The New Normal*. He led me to a bulletin board in the kitchen. There, pinned in the middle, was my note. He'd saved it all this time.

That gesture gave me an inkling of the man I was dealing with, one with a steel-trap mind, a feverish creativity, and a superhuman attention to detail. "All good things come from detail," he said. Those qualities had led him to the pinnacle of power in television, a scrappy fighter in a business not for the faint of heart. Now he and I were in the process of the delicate dance every designer does with a prospective client: how far to go in terms of a renovation?

Ryan led, of course. But the house in question was very much a blank slate. It was a huge and ungainly structure built in the 1990s on a sizable parcel in the Pacific Palisades. Ryan had already begun to strip its 10,000 square feet of large rooms with high ceilings to the bare bones. With the preservation of the footprint of the house as the only mandate, there was every indication that this was to be a near-total architectural restructuring.

When I came into the picture, there were a couple of existing elements that provided inspiration. Ryan had already begun placing enormous steel casement windows and doors throughout the house. This aesthetic, typical of the homes of the 1920s, gave the house a powerful and timeless solidity. Generations to come would be looking out those windows, I thought.

This particular enclave in Pacific Palisades, however, is rich in history, with no street lamps or sidewalks and the clip clop of horse's hooves in a country atmosphere just off of Sunset Boulevard. So I nodded in assent when Ryan, in his usual infectious manner, mentioned *The Big Valley*, the 1960s Barbara Stanwyck TV horse opera, as a launching point. He wasn't talking of the Victorian mansion over which she lorded, but rather its lush, romantic, and epic sweep. It brought to my mind a term, *grounded fabulosity*, which was used to describe Ryan in a *New Yorker* magazine profile. He admitted to the writer that his taste was "baroque," not in the ornate sense of the word but meaning that he took "a maximalist approach to storytelling."

This was evident in his total love of process. Whatever I sent to him was carefully considered and analyzed. Such was the case with the book on the architect Irving S. Gill, which I felt could be an important lodestar for the project. A modernist take on Spanish Colonia revival, Gill's métier was simplicity, restraint and a rigorous adherence to rules. Beauty emanated from shapes and graphic silhouettes and the surfaces and materials would be limited: white stucco, dark oak, black stone, wrought iron. It might seem a stretch that someone with a maximalist approach would respond to such an ethic. But Ryan was highly sensitive to design, form and theme and he loved rigor. He immediately recognized Gill's playbook as a way to bring symmetry and clarity to the disjointed architecture.

Nowhere was application of this aesthetic more essential than at the problematic entrance. It was quite a trek from the road to the front door and a disorienting one at that. You had to navigate a series of awkward steps through a tower that was off the axis from the main house and which then led into an unappealing courtyard. The challenge was to make sense of it spatially by creating what architects refer to as "a path of desire," an engaging and pleasurable sense of direction, as innate to people as to animals.

To establish a sense of flow—literally and figuratively—we were both enthused over the idea of fountains, as many as possible. I designed parallel, 30-foot long rectangular fountains leading visitors to the tower which held guest rooms, a bar, and a bathroom. Once through that passageway, I added a round courtyard fountain on the same axis as the tower to serve as a focal point. Since the front door was askew from that line of vision, I suggested to Ryan an all-encompassing semi-circle of steps—an amphitheater, if you will—which would lead to the courtyard and provide an easily navigable "path of desire" to the front door. He said, "No."

Coming into the process as a director, Ryan was always quick, decisive and intensely organized. I got the answers I needed, if not necessarily the answers I wanted. I took it seriously when he fought against my ideas. After all, this was a guy who was expert at evoking a period. You only had to look at the hotel and asylum in his American Horror Story. When a client rejects a proposal, I can often rethink it and come up with another version. In this case, however, I felt this architectural element was a strong solution to the entrance. I persisted. And he pushed right back.

"I know you think it's a bad idea, but the entrance sets the tone and the steps will tie everything together spatially," I explained. I sensed him weakening. It was not something he did often so I bided my time, looking for any opening to press my case. Finally, he said with some exasperation, "Okay, Stephen, go ahead and do your amphitheater." My stubbornness was eventually vindicated. I smiled to myself when I later heard he'd said to Beth Cowan, our project manager, "I fought Stephen so hard on this and he prevailed. And he was right."

Like Diane, and unlike some clients, Ryan never deviated from the ground rules we set down. So as the project developed, it took on that classic modernism which had made Irving Gill such a celebrated architect. The simplicity extended to the multiples of fireplaces grandfathered into the house and the arches that we refined to establish a unity as you went from room to room. Ryan had a fondness for the fireplaces at the Roxbury house so we re-created those and used the same brick—Diane's long sought-after "perfect brick"—on the terrace and in other parts of the exterior.

The graphic quality associated with modernism was most present in the risers to the steps. They were typically multicolored in old Spanish Colonial homes but when I suggested that the design be in black and white and gray, Ryan one-upped me: "Let's just do black and white," he said. It made for an appealing, if extremely graphic design. I did five different versions of the simplest geometric angles I could find and we alternated those throughout the house and in the exterior. It made for a "wow" effect.

The white stucco walls, dark oak beams, and black stone floors gave the house an almost monastic feel, a purity emphasized by Ryan's insistence that the walls remain unadorned by art. It was less Barbara Stanwyck and more ecclesiastical, which wasn't surprising since in the *New Yorker* article, Ryan had expressed his youthful ambition to one day be Pope. The truth of the matter is that for all the indications Ryan gave of being the powerful television mogul he most certainly is, he could also surprise me. At one point early in the process, as we were surveying the structure, he suddenly piped up, "You know what? I've always wanted a great laundry room!" And that is how a laundry of epic scale came to the Pacific Palisades. Who would have thought his grounded fabulosity would extend to laundry rooms?

The more expected variant on that fabulousness came when we were examining fonts for a gigantic black wrought-iron M to place on the exterior white stucco wall off the bedroom. It was Ryan's nod to Diane's love of graphic imagery, an example of which was the steel we'd bent and forged to form the address, 820 Roxbury Drive, on the house he'd purchased from her. As we looked at fonts, Ryan had another idea. "What about putting, 'Oh, California!' on the courtyard wall?" he said with that Murphy gleam in his eye. It was from a song by one his favorite artists, Joni Mitchell.

"Oh, California
Oh will you take me as I am?
Will you take me as I am?
Will you?"

Ryan had chanced on the perfect epilogue for our monumental undertaking. With its 30-foot bubbling fountains, looming amphitheater entrance, massive wood doors, and pure white walls, there was a monumentality that fused the past with the future. Looking at it, I could trace a line from Flash Gordon to Oz to Metropolis, all those cinematic visions fixed somewhere between earth and pure imagination. That is what my collaboration with Ryan had been—as with my other clients who'd been driven to tell narratives on screen and, as well, through their homes. What a privilege to have indulged in those fantasies with them. A dream factory in and of itself.

"Oh, California!"

Indeed.

Interior furnishing by Studio Shamshiri

WILFRED BUCKLAND
2035 PINEHURST ROAD
HOLLYWOOD, CALIF.

Mr Ray Haner

Leeds,

Greene Co.,

New York.

Ruins of Potic Castle after fire (top); Wilfred Buckland letter
1939, Hollywood (center); Potic Castle, ca. 1913 (bottom);

My great-grandfather, Martin Stuben-rauch, in his eighties, had been sitting and looking off into nothingness when his wife, Adeline, asked "Martin, what are you doing?" He replied, "Ach, Mama, I'm just building air castles." After decades of imagining my own air castles, that story came back to me when I finally set about building the real thing.

Well, not exactly a castle, but that is what my home is known as: Potic Castle. It was given that name by the locals when it first rose in 1913 on a cliff overlooking a broad valley and the purpled majesty of the Catskill Mountains. Designed by Wilfred Buckland in an English Arts and Crafts style, the three-story stone and shingle structure had been commissioned as

Stephen's concept drawing of a rebuilt Potic Castle

a summer refuge for British sisters, Katharine and Elizabeth Grier. Decades later, the home was all but laid waste as a result of a devastating fire in the 1970s. So when I first came upon the site what remained were the stone foundation and two chimneys. I became obsessed after uncovering some vintage photographs of the place and learned the colorful history that linked Buckland to Hollywood. Starting out as a Broadway set designer, he went out West and teamed up with the legendary director-producer Cecil B. DeMille as production and lighting designer for his early silent films. In fact, Potic once served as a setting for a 1924 silent movie, *Icebound*, directed by DeMille's brother, William.

I managed to purchase the property and proceeded to design my dream home on the massive stone foundation. My idea was simple, honor the particular genius of the past and carry it into the future. Using the ruins and old photographs as my template, I decided to duplicate the original exterior as an homage to Buckland and yet create my own unique environment inside. Buckland's approach had been idiosyncratic and so would be mine, a blend of industrial functionality and rough-hewn dark wood cabinetry. As I started the design process, I knew exactly the person to call: my old friend and mentor, designer Bob Bray.

We soon agreed the dominant theme of the interior would be to evoke the spirit of an old lodge. I'd long admired the great style and comfort of those found in the national parks. Browsing a book of Adirondack homes, we were captivated by a dark shingled structure with windows painted a vivid red. I suggested the sashes of the casement windows be painted what Frank Lloyd Wright dubbed Cherokee Red. From that scheme came the idea of concrete floors the same color. When I told Bob that I wanted windows on either side of the entrance, he balked.

"Don't do it," he said.

"Why?" I responded.

"It's a castle, you want it to be a fortress," he said. "You don't want to reveal the magic of that view until people walk through the door."

Bob, as usual, was right. Part of the drama of the house also came from the massive boulders of blue-stone, excavated from blasting into the mountain,

which I installed in the entrance and in front of the fireplace. They gave the appearance of the earth itself erupting into the rooms and, with their myriad tiny fossils, served as reminders of the millennia which had formed the surrounding terrain. I also retained the scorched patina on the brick fireplaces, a memento of the house's fiery past, around which I rebuilt the many rooms.

The furnishings in the house give me away as a packrat, the contents curated as a veritable guidebook of my travels, from pillows hand-sewn by my mother Dorothy, to the antique Japanese iron lanterns I had recast for one of Jennifer Aniston's homes. Potic is replete with finds I picked up while touring with Disney: an old roll-top desk in a guest room, a little art nouveau brass ash tray, and a weathered mechanic's chest which once belonged to legendary race car driver Barney Oldfield. There is also a tiny herd of cast-iron buffalo on a mantle in my bedroom complementing the many Edward Curtis prints of Native American culture throughout the house. I am in the process of painting murals in the living room, oil on canvas, drawn from nineteenth-century photographs of Hudson Valley rural vistas not unlike the those captured by artists Thomas Cole and Frederick Edwin Church.

The nexus of past and present is perhaps best experienced at Potic in an aged and over-sized leather-bound book which once served as a guest register for the Players West Room, a private club for Hollywood actors and their fellow travelers. Its large yellowed pages are filled with countless signatures of celebrities, including the elegant cursive of a 17-year-old Elizabeth Taylor. I discovered it collecting dust, forgotten on an upper shelf of a prop room at one of the studios where I once worked as a scenic artist. Particularly touching is the inaugural entry by actress Beulah Bondi, who chose on August 3, 1942, to quote from a poem, "Time can claim no victory o'er the heart."

The book now serves as Potic Castle's own record of visitors. And while many of the present inscriptions are less poetic, they are nonetheless, just as heartfelt.

Stephen painting a backdrop, Morningside High School, 1964

In Sum/Acknowledgments

STEPHEN SHADLEY

For Diane Keaton who, over the years, changed the trajectory of my life with her ideas, support and abiding friendship.

For the eloquence, determination and patience of my friend Patrick Pacheco, who chronicled my stories and brought them to life.

For Charles Meirs for taking a chance on me with this book and for the unerring and patient guidance of editor Douglas Curran. For the creative vision of art director Gabriele Wilson whose design brought a disparate body of work together seamlessly and artfully.

For the artists, whose faith in me and friendship made a career possible: Diane Keaton, Jennifer Aniston, Ryan Murphy, Matthew Modine, Woody Allen and Robert Altman. For Paige Rense, Amy Astley, Alison Levasseur and so many friends at *Architectural Digest* over the years. For Richard Gillette and the design partnership we forged for nearly a decade.

For my brother, John Shadley, and my extended family, throughout life, who continue to inspire me in countless ways: Clay Beale, Tim Hawkins, David Glomb, Marcello Villano, Bob Bray, Thad Hayes, Warren Battle, Carol Kane, Tom Nardini, Susan Lange, Michael Murphy, Marylou Luther and Dorrie Hall. For the brilliant photographers whose work appears throughout these pages: David Glomb, Steve Gross and Sue Daley, David Miller, Tim Street-Porter, Scott Frances, Jaime Ardiles-Arce, Michael Mundy, Erhard Pfeiffer, Mary Nichols, Peter Vitale and Rick Gillette.

First published in the United States of America in 2020
by RIZZOLI INTERNATIONAL PUBLICATIONS, INC.
300 Park Avenue South, New York, NY 10010
www.rizzoliusa.com

© 2020 Rizzoli International Publications, Inc.
Text © 2020 Stephen Shadley

Publisher: Charles Miers
Editor: Douglas Curran
Production Manager: Alyn Evans
Managing Editor: Lynn Scrabis

Designed by Gabriele Wilson

Printed and bound in China

2020 2021 2022 2023 2024/ 10 9 8 7 6 5 4 3 2 1

ISBN-13: 978-0-8478-6659-5
Library of Congress Control Number: 2020937848

Visit us online:
Facebook.com/RizzoliNewYork
Twitter: @Rizzoli_Books
Instagram.com/RizzoliBooks
Pinterest.com/RizzoliBooks
Youtube.com/user/RizzoliNY
Issuu.com/Rizzoli

MOVIE HOUSES PHOTOGRAPHY CREDITS

page 2:	DAVID GLOMB
page 6:	STEVE GROSS AND SUSAN DALEY
pages 8-9:	DAVID CLAYTON MILLER
page 10:	TIM STREET-PORTER
page 15:	PORTRAIT: RICK GILLETTE
page 17:	POSTER DESIGN: APRIL SILVER, PHOTO: JAMIE SPRACHTER
pages 19-20	DAVID GLOMB
page 21:	PETER VITALE
pages 25-33:	MICHAEL MUNDY
pages 34-43:	JAIME ARDILES-ARCE
pages 44-59:	DAVID GLOMB
pages 60-73:	JAIME ARDILES-ARCE
pages 74-75:	DAVID GLOMB
pages 76-83:	TIM STREET-PORTER
page 84:	DAVID GLOMB
page 85:	TIM STREET-PORTER
page 86:	DAVID GLOMB
pages 87-91:	TIM STREET-PORTER
pages 92-93:	MARY E. NICHOLS
page 94:	ERHARD PFEIFFER
pages 96-97:	MARY E. NICHOLS
page 98-99:	ERHARD PFEIFFER
pages 100-121:	TIM STREET-PORTER
pages 122-139:	STEVE GROSS AND SUSAN DALEY
pages 140-161:	DAVID GLOMB
pages 162-173:	SCOTT FRANCES
pages 174-176:	DAVID GLOMB
page 177:	JOHNNY CARSON, GETTY IMAGES®
pages 178-191:	DAVID GLOMB
pages 192-211:	DAVID CLAYTON MILLER
page 212:	RUIN: STEVE GROSS AND SUSAN DALEY
pages 214-221:	STEVE GROSS AND SUSAN DALEY